"When the time is right all things are released from their hidden places and brought to the light of day."

DREAM FEATHER

Viento Stan-Padilla

Dawne-Leigh Publications

Dawne-Leigh Publications
231 Adrian Road
Millbrae, California 94030

Distributed by Atheneum Publishers
597 Fifth Avenue
New York, NY 10017

★ Manufactured in the United States of America ★

Library of Congress Cataloging in Publication Data

Stan-Padilla, Viento, 1945 -
    Dream feather.

    1. Stan-Padilla, Viento, 1945 -   2. Yaqui Indians — Art.   3. Yaqui Indians — Religion and mythology.   4. Indians of North America — Religion and mythology.   5. Spiritual life.   6. Indians of North America — Art.
    I. Title.
    E99.Y3S79   299'.7   79-26213
    ISBN 0-89742-035-7

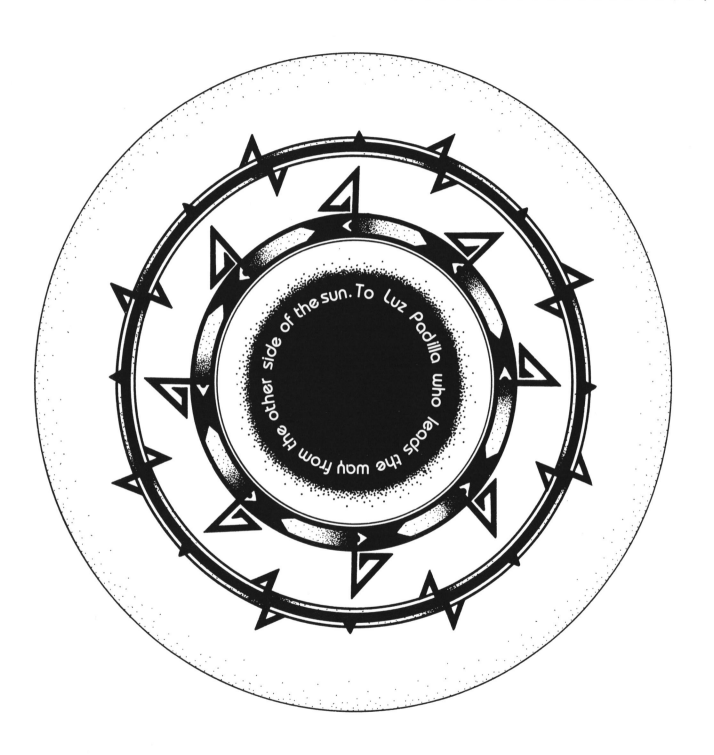

the other side of the sun. To Luz Padilla who leads the way from

THE SOURCE

As the clouds on the horizon,
forms come and go and come again.
Seasons come and go and the rhythms
and cycles of nature hide the ancient
treasures of the past and give them
life on the new horizon.

The luminous constellations of the past
disappear and come again embodied in
new forms.
The symbols etched in stone record
this truth.

The source is the Creator,
an infinite being, and is the essence
and potential of all living forms.
In its purity it is self-existent and
carries the universe in all
dimensions and all directions.
Its breath gave light to the darkness
releasing into each thing unfolding
motion,
So that the circle of life
would be unbroken.

Above us all is the long living
   spirit of the sun
whose glowing strands weave us together,
   generation after generation.

Into each age one is chosen
   to carry the seed,
   which is the breath of the future.

Dream Feather is the story of
   the planting of that seed.

DREAM FEATHER

In the stillness of the mountain world
    the darkness lay cold and closed
    in secret mystery.
The morning light softened
    the mountain tops and
    lifted the darkness from the crevices
    and wrinkles of stone.

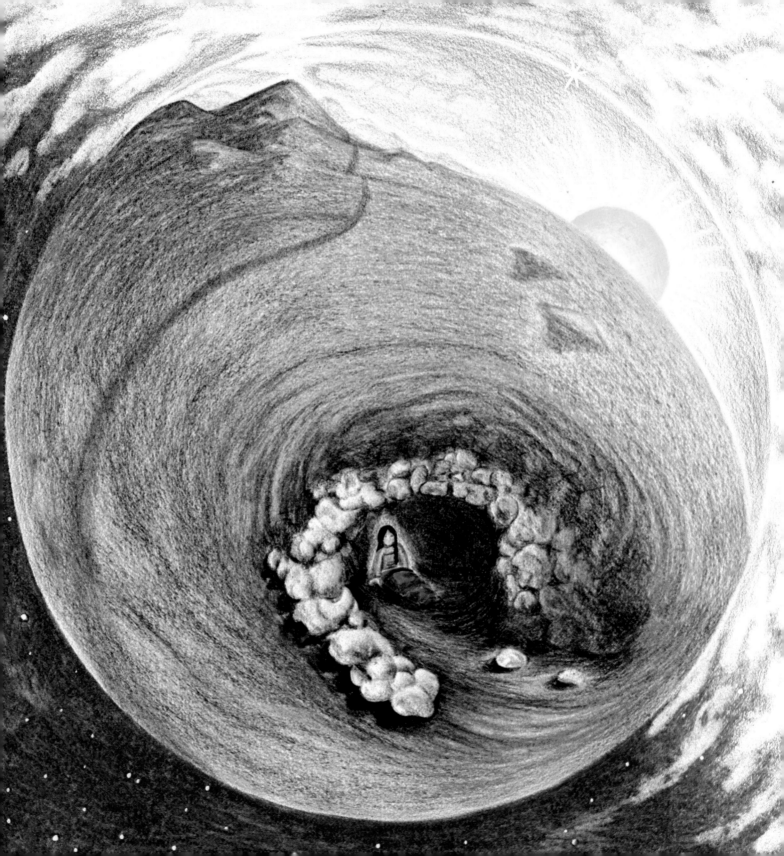

From the white silence
        the Sun shared its brilliant song.
The song drifted downward
        tone upon tone,
        guided by a feather.

Stirring to the morning song
    the boy saw the movement of the
    Dream Feather.
Sitting up, he knew that this was a day
    that had been long awaited.

From the long past the Grandfathers'
    voices filled the space around him,
    chanting the stories of a journey.
The journey that he was to take.

The rare power of the Sun's song
    could not be understood by words alone
    but he knew from the Grandfathers
    and the ancient stone etchings
    on the cave walls
    that the feather was foretold and
    would be his guide.
He was to follow it and
    return to the source.

Ancient memories flowed through the boy
    and he stood to reach for the feather.
His journey began through earth and stone
    and was made easy for him by his
    secret understanding that
    when the time is right all
    things are released from their
    hidden places
    and brought to the light of day.

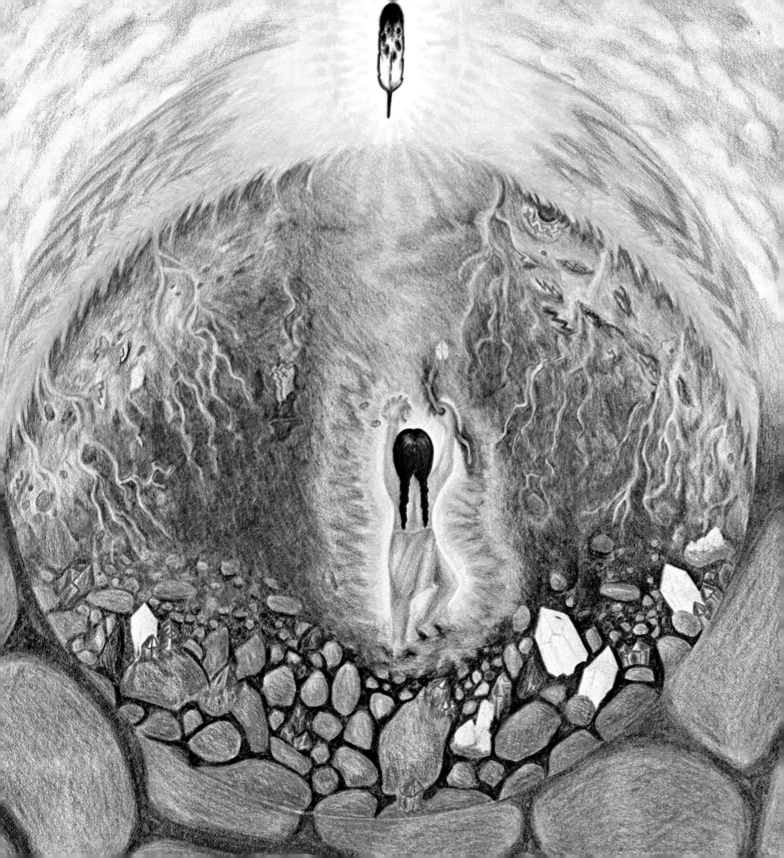

Through a shower of corn pollen
    they broke from the earth's surface,
drawn upward by the wind's breath
    and the Dream Feather humming
    in the current of the sky's stream.

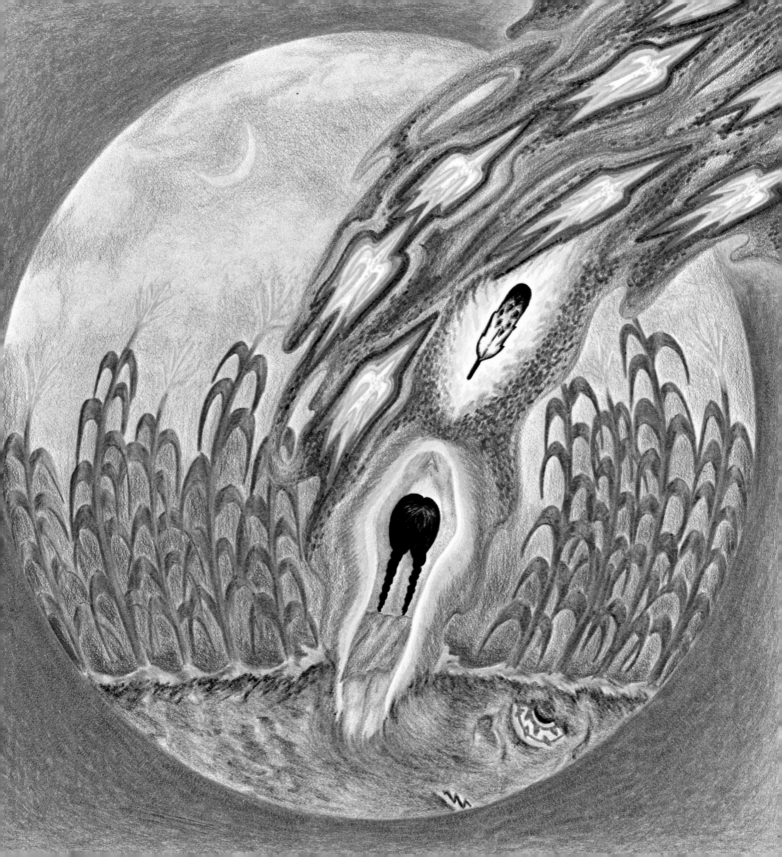

He was soaring above the earth
with the spirit wind, moving
toward a rainbow cloud
that pulsed with music
of every hue, and rang clear
tones from its crystal heart.

In the cloud world the boy followed
   the feather through the crystalline mist,
   toward the center that was hidden from the
   world below.
At the center was the spiraling
   pattern of the ancient song
   radiating like a jewel.

Through the jewel he could
   see a path of six steps.
Each step a pure color,
   each step a note in the ancient song.

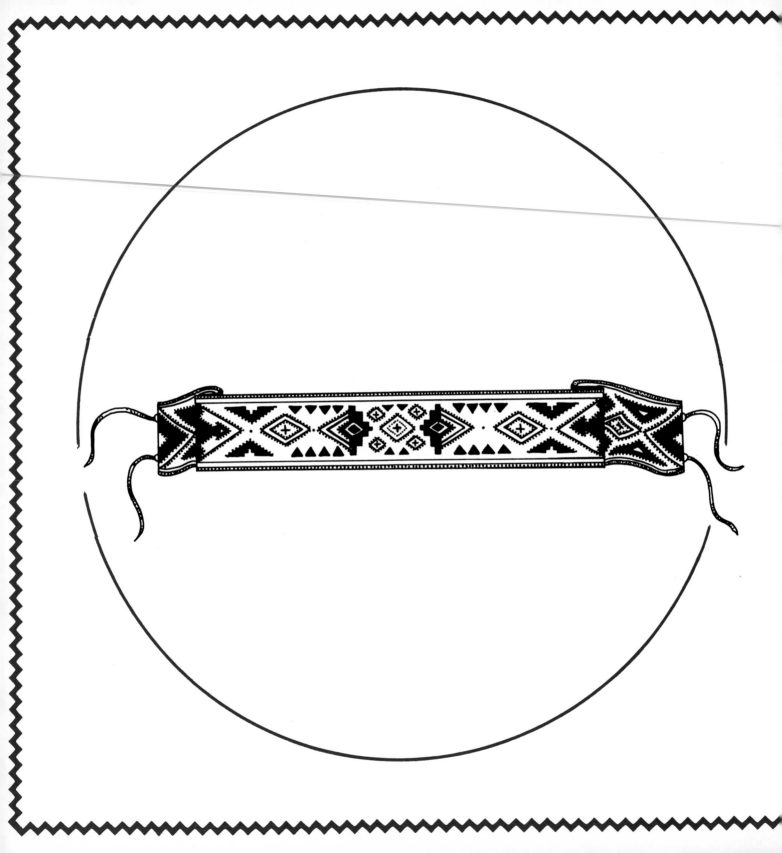

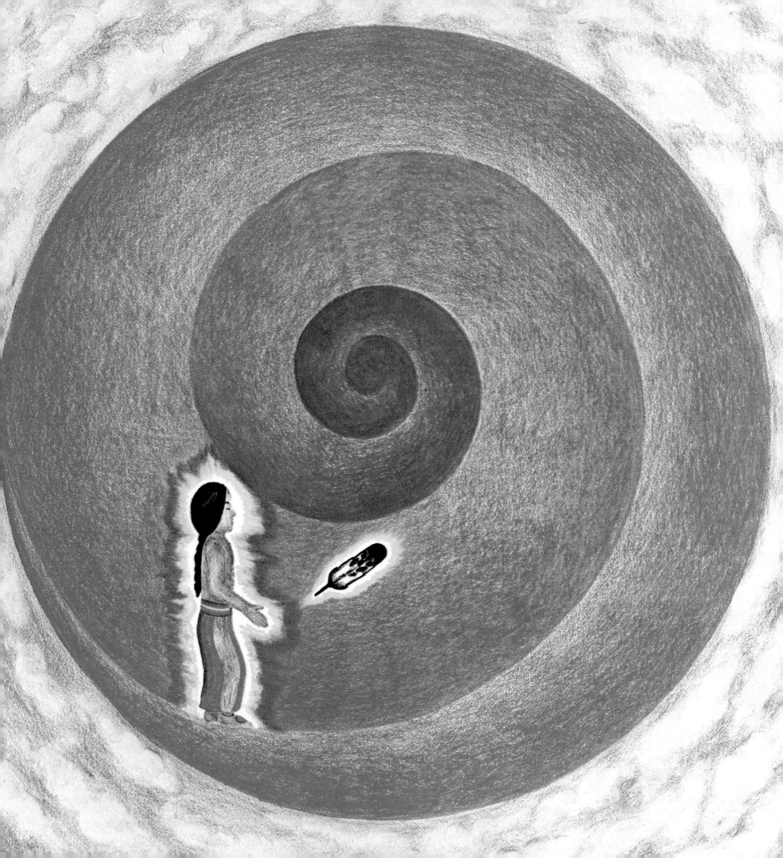

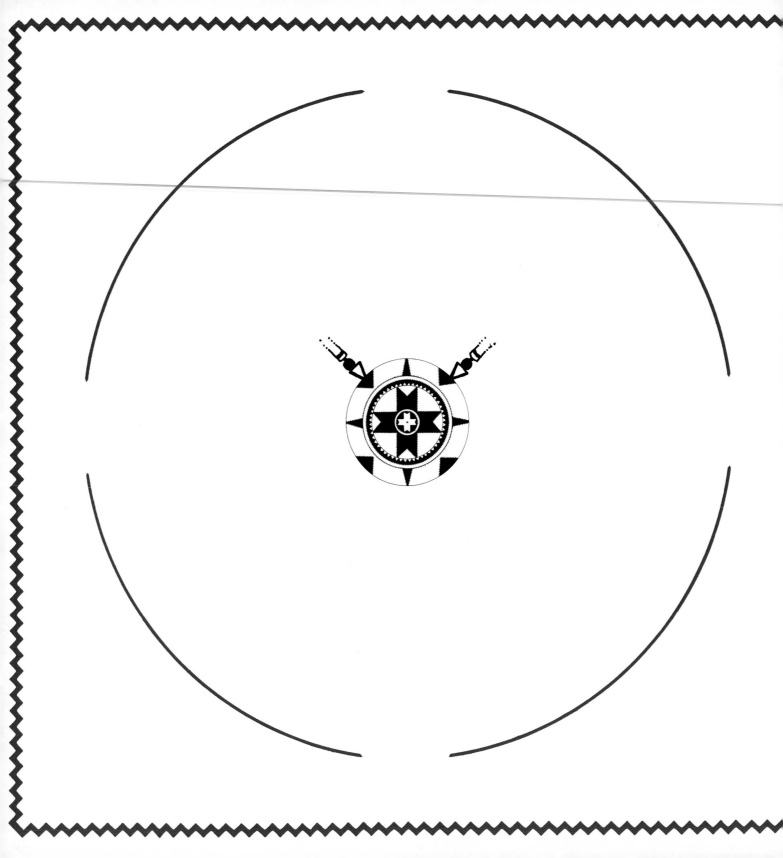

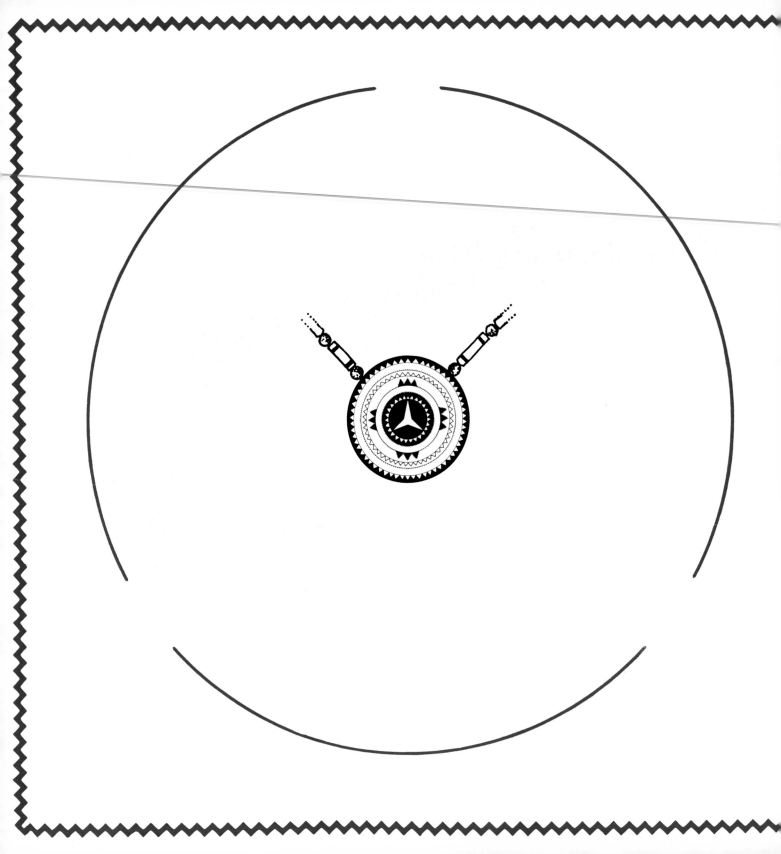

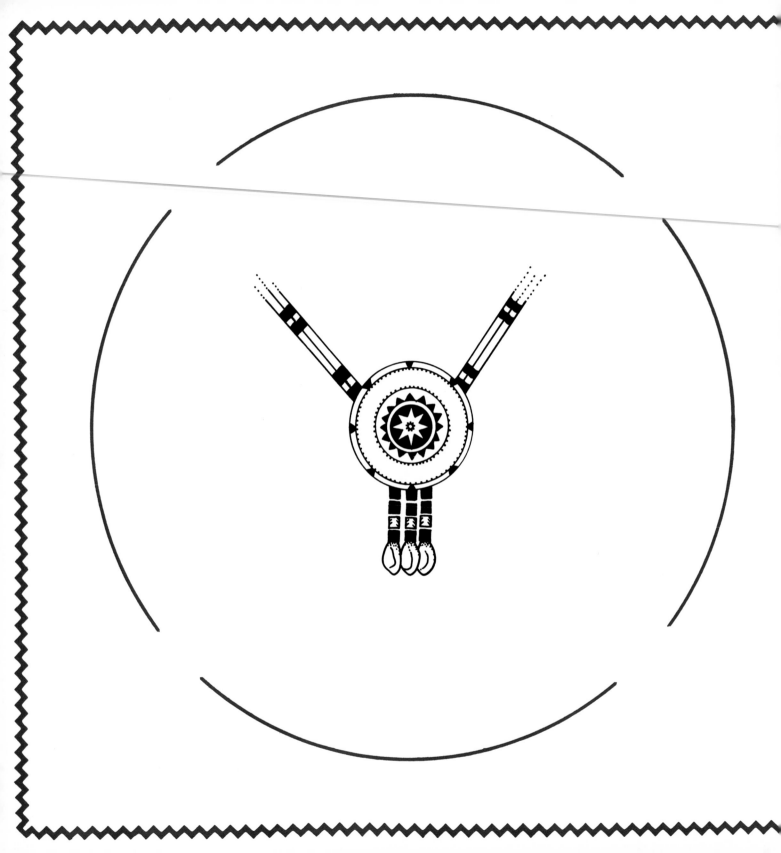

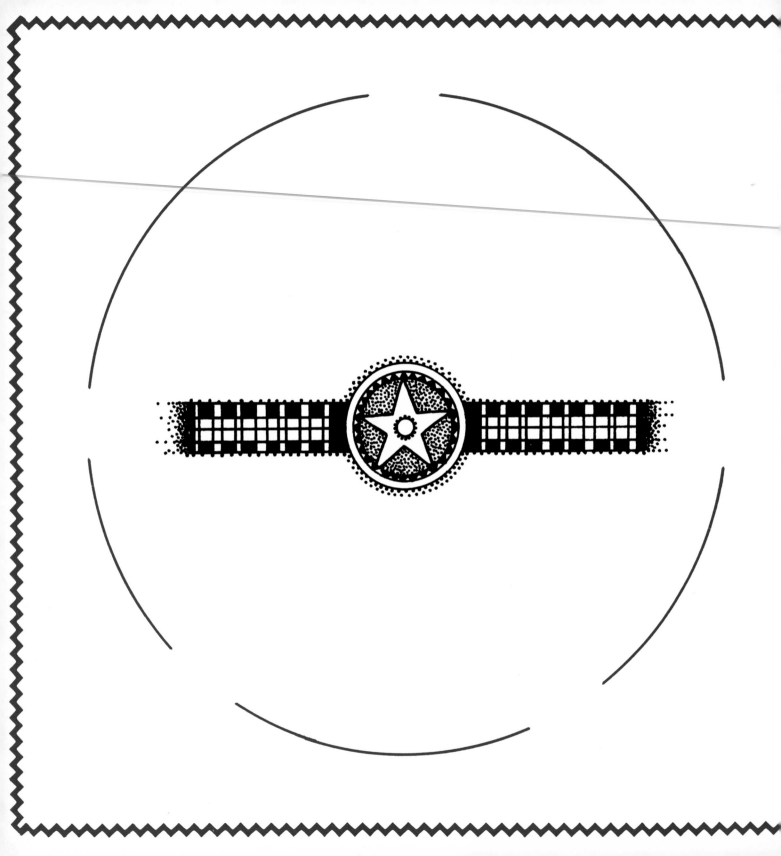

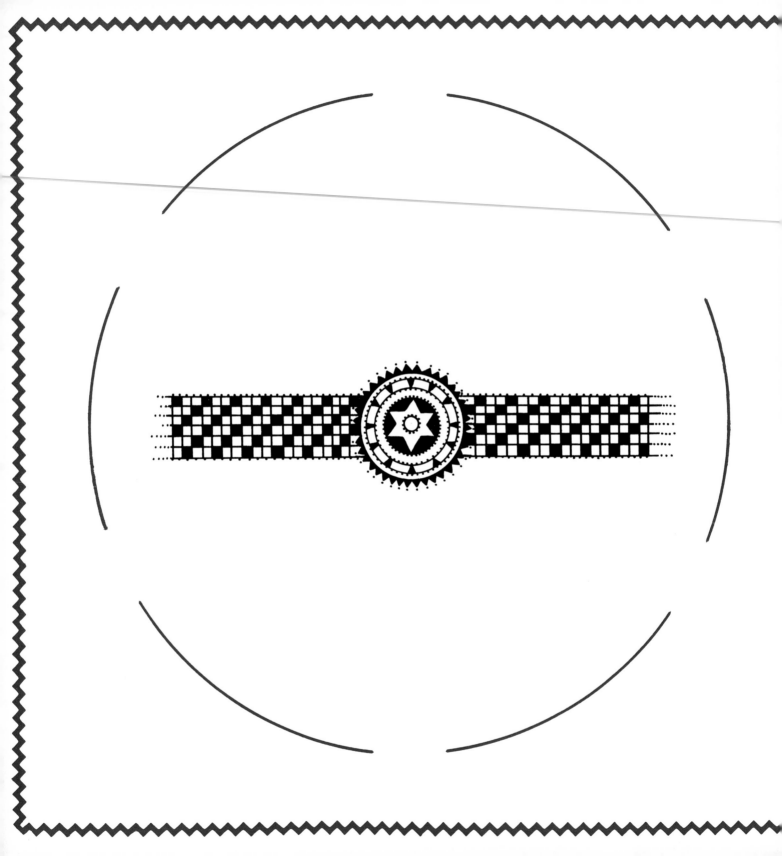

The boy emerged from the
    crystalline mist singing
    the ancient song and clothed
    from the spiral steps.
In an instant the music stilled
    to the white silence —
    the center of the Sun —
    till the spiral released him
    toward the other side.

Flying free, his face reflected
    the purest light and
    the brightest of all —
The light of the Crystal Star.

The boy glowed at the threshold
    of the shining presence.
His heart vibrated with an
    inner light made brighter
    by the flame.
The flame that held the seed,
    the seed that was placed
    at the center of his heart.

Fire, flash and brilliant light,
Illumination shot through true prism,
    reunited and fused forever to
    the circle of creation.
The circle that revolves with time,
    ageless as dreams, dreams of plantings
    and harvests, of seasons, journeys,
    and returning home.

THE RETURN

The cave within the heart of the sacred mountain
   glowed with a clear light.
It was dressed to welcome the boy
   from his journey and waited
   in its stillness for his voice.

''I am awake; I have returned
   from my dream.
What was placed in my heart
   is also in my mind.
My mind and my heart remember as one.
The feather that was my guide
   now leads my hand as it did once my dream.
It asks me to take its name,
   and from this time my name is Dream Feather.''

The chorus of Grandfathers sang
    the name of Dream Feather.
They also sang to him saying,

        "It is for the planting in this
            season we celebrate,
            and for all those who will
            breathe the fragrance of a
            future flowering.
            The seed must have many to care for it.
    Listen, and you will hear
            its heartbeat in the earth,
            feel its warmth beneath your feet.
            Tend the seasons with gentleness
            and prepare for the time of your journey.
    Watch for a Dream Feather
            and join the circle.
            When all in each generation have done so,
            the wheel of light will be complete."

Dream Feather walked from
the cave of secrets
out upon the earth.
The flame in his heart
shone through his eyes
as he greeted the Sun
with a smile.

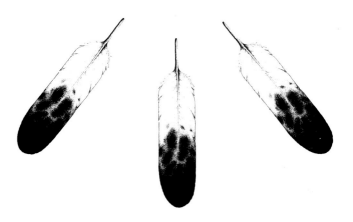

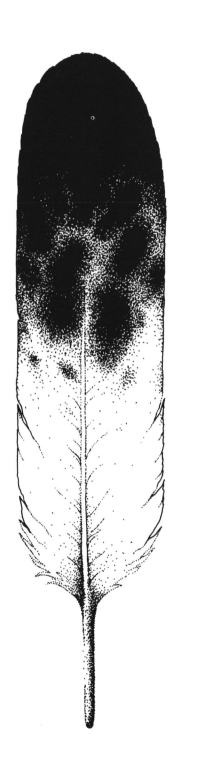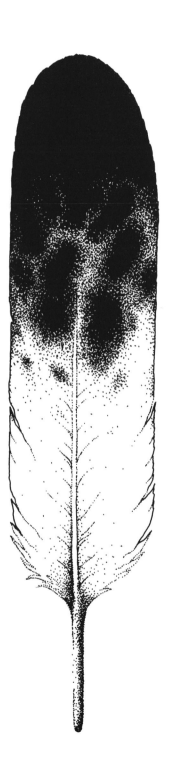